BERMUDA

TRIANGLE

Bermuda Triangle is an interesting play that chronicles the adventures of a group of friends after they are transported to a different world. They have to make life-changing decisions while maintaining their sanity, in order to make it back to their own world.

Bermuda Triangle

BY

FEMI ONI

For additional copies of this or other Femi Oni titles write:

Korloki Publishing Company (A subsidiary of Allzents Groups Inc.,)

P.O. Box 300605 Brooklyn, NY 11230

Please allow 2-3 weeks for delivery.

For bulk orders contact us via

Email kpcbooks@yahoo.com

Copyright © 2012 Femi Oni/ Korloki Publishing Company
BERMUDA TRIANGLE

Request for information should be addressed to
Korloki Publishing Company
P.O. Box 300605
Brooklyn, NY 11230

All rights reserved. No part of the author's original material may be reproduced, stored in a retrieval system or transmitted in any form or by any means – electronics, mechanical, photocopy, recording or any other –except for brief quotations in printed review, without the prior permission of the publisher.

Cover design by: Sel P.
Interior design: Korloki Graphics Inc.
Summary: Fantasy and Adventures

ISBN: 13   978-1-936-739-16-5

ISBN: 10   1936739165

PRINTED IN THE UNITED STATES OF AMERICA

DEDICATION

Dedicated to my parents, Mr. and Mrs. Oni.

Bermuda Triangle

BY

FEMI ONI

INTRODUCTION

Bermuda Triangle **is** an intriguing fantasy tale that sets you off on an exciting adventure with a group of friends sucked into a different and harsh world. They have to use their wits to survive and have to make life-changing decisions in order to make it back to their own world.

Sit back and enjoy the magic!

-Femi Oni

June 1, 2012

15th October 2020

It is noon; six FedEx officials are on a yacht sailing back to Florida. Mark a young man; Amanda a pretty looking young lady and Joey a man of average height are lying on their backs enjoying the warmth of the sun when Stingas, an averagely built man about 6ft tall comes out of the cabin

Stingas

What a magnificent sunset on a beautiful evening

Amanda

You can't get anything better (*as she pours from the bottle of champagne*) *After a short pause* .... where are Kelly and Fergie?

Stingas

They are in the cabin

Amanda

Why not call them to come out here?

Fergie, a handsome man with straw colored long hair and Kelly, a woman with strawberry blond hair, come out of the cabin laughing with half-filled glasses of champagne in their hands.

Fergie

I'm on cloud nine right now (*he belches loudly, sounding drunk*)

Stingas

You are getting tipsy and I think you have had enough to drink (*as he collects*

the glass from Fergie's hands) ....
remember you are the sailor of this yacht

Fergie

I got everything under control *(he mutters)*

..... some moments later they all fall asleep except for Stingas who is leaning on the railings watching the ocean tides. Suddenly he stands up straight looking baffled like he has seen something strange.

Stingas

Wake up Fergie!! (*he screams*) .... wake up everybody!!!.......I think we're headed for the triangle

Fergie

What triangle? (*he mutters from his sleep*)

The others are awake and are already running towards Stingas to see what is going on.

Joey

I think he is right *(as he runs to Fergie and pulls him up)* .... come on! Wake up! Don't get us killed, man. You need to steer us out of here *(he yells)*

By this time, the yacht is in a whirlpool and the ship is swerving uncontrollably. Fergie gets up quickly and runs into the cabin. He grabs the steering wheel and tries to take control of the yacht but it is too late.

They all begin to scream and yell.

FADE OUT

FADE IN

They are all lying on a desert unconscious. The desert looks very strange; the sky is like a flowing river and it seemed as if they were beneath the water. Sounds of squeaking birds can be heard. Stingas opens his eyes slowly and immediately gets up upon sighting the strange land they are in. The others wake up in turn.

Mark

Where are we?

Joey

We must be in the triangle (*as he dusts the sand from his shirt*)

Kelly

We are never going to get out of here (*crying*)

Stingas

Relax! Let's calm down and find out where we are first

Joey

Fergie, this is all your fault (*he pushes Fergie on the chest and Fergie pushes him back*)

Mark

This is no time for an argument, we have a situation here. We don't even know where we are and all you two can do is fight and argue (*he says angrily*)

Suddenly they hear the whistling of a very strong wind.

Stingas

Come on! (*as he runs towards the forest ahead of them with the others running after him. They are soon in the woods of the forest where they sit on an enormous fallen tree limb. They are all breathing heavily. Suddenly, they hear the wind blowing in their direction, quite close to them.*

Mark

The wind! It's coming

He gets up from the tree limb and begins to run further into the woods with the others running after him. After some time, the wind stops blowing and then they hear a soft voice whispering.

Voice

I am the wind of direction and I was only doing my job

Frightened, they listened as the voice spoke.

Stingas

Who are you? And where are we? We can't even see you, come out

Voice

You cannot see a wind; all you should do is follow the narrow path ahead

The wind blows away from the forest.

Mark

I think we have no other choice but to follow that path. It seems like the only option here

They continue moving along the path which leads to a hill. They walk up the hill and after a long while, they hear the voices of people chanting. Puzzled and

frightened, they stand still and keep quiet.

They see a troop of soldiers running down a valley, about a thousand of them, with swords in their hands. They all have blue hair, sharply pointed noses and ears and are dressed like warriors from ancient times. The soldiers move on towards the deep of the forest. Mark and the others hide behind a big tree until the soldiers have gone then they continue to wander along.

Joey

Where could they be going to or where could they be coming from?

Mark

They must have a kingdom somewhere

Joey

Who knows? They might be friendly, show us some hospitality and show us the way out of here

Stingas

Those people didn't look friendly, rather they looked mean

Fergie

Looks can be deceptive. However those people looked like soldiers and soldiers are usually mean

Soon, they come across a small wooden cottage in the deep of the forest.

Joey

That's a house! I knew people would live around here. I just knew it!

Fergie

Let's sneak around and find out. I hope we find something to eat as I'm really hungry

Amanda

I'm hungry too

They sneak towards the cottage; Joey peeps inside through the window and sees a table, a chair and a two-seater couch but there is no one to be seen inside.

Joey

No one is inside, let's find the door

They stealthily move along the wall of the cottage towards the front. When they turn around the cottage, they come in view of a big farmland full of different kinds of fruits.

Kelly

Wow!!!

Fergie

This is what I'm talking about (*as he runs towards the farm and grabs an apple*)

They all rush on to the farmland plucking off fruits and voraciously eating them. After they have eaten to their satisfaction, they begin to store some of the fruits in their pockets and then they resume on their journey.

Moments after they leave, a dwarf named Krumpy with blue hair, pointed nose and ears and carrying a big sack on his back, approaches the farm. As soon as he reaches the farm, he knows someone has been there. He rushes into his cottage and drops the sack on the floor.

Dwarf

I must send a message to Gatalina as fast as possible (*in a croaky voice*)

Meanwhile, the crew seems to have arrived at the end of the path; where they come across another wooden cottage.

Joey

I guess there must be another farmland here

Kelly

I have already finished all my fruits. I really hope we will get some more here

Stingas

Well, we will soon find out (*he approaches the cottage with the others following a step behind him*)

The front door to the cottage is wide open.

Mark

The door is open, someone might be in there

Stingas

Let's check

Fergie

No way am I going in there with you …… a monster could be in there!

Stingas walks in the door slowly, with the others creeping behind him. Inside the cottage are a big rocking chair and a table on which a jug and a mug lie.

There is a fireplace in the corner of the room.

Mark

Someone surely lives here (*quietly*)

Amanda

But I don't think there's any one at home

There is a door on the left side of the room. Stingas walks up and quietly opens it; inside is a kitchen with pots hanging on the wall and fruits on the kitchen table. They walk in and Joey quickly grabs an orange.

Joey

I'm famished! (*as he takes a bite*)

Suddenly they hear a rattling sound coming from the outside.

Kelly

What's that sound? (*looking frightened*)

Stingas creeps to the front door to look and sees a man coming. The man is very old, with black hair and a long black beard. The man walks into the cottage while Stingas hurries back into the kitchen and closes the kitchen door slowly.

Stingas

Be quiet (*he whispers*)

The old man has just sat down on the rocking chair to relax when Fergie mistakenly hits a saucepan hanging on the wall with his head and it falls to the ground. The old man looks towards the kitchen and draws a sword from under the chair. He moves closer and opens the kitchen door slowly with his sword pointing inside. Stingas quickly hits the sword with a sauce pan and grapples with the old man.

Stingas

Who are you? (*he shouts out as he struggles to get the sword away from the man*)

After a couple of minutes in which both men struggle and roll around on the floor, the sword falls down and Mark quickly takes hold of it.

Mark

Tell us who you are (*pointing the sword at the old man's forehead*)

Old Man

I'll explain if you would just let me go.
My name is Johnson

Stingas lets go off the man.

Johnson

Let's all sit down. I mean you no harm.
Let's get something to eat while we talk

The old man gathers some food, enough for everyone to eat. They follow him outside the house where he builds a fire. Then they all sit around the fire and commence eating.

Johnson

I am Johnson, a victim of the Bermuda trap. Many humans are trapped here as well and are being held hostage by the Gatalinans. I managed to escape from the prison during a festival; at the time when the prisoners are brought out to watch the festival. I escaped with the help of a guard whose life my father had once saved on the fields when he almost fell off a cliff. He let me escape as a sign of gratitude

Kelly

Gatalinans? Who are they?

Johnson

This is the kingdom of Gatalina. The king is very powerful and has about ten thousand soldiers in his army. The soldiers often come into the forest to drink from a waterfall as the water from there makes them powerful to fight and win any battle. They also have a trap farm which attracts any new stranger to the kingdom. Once any stranger eats any fruit on the farm, the farm custodian knows immediately. He quickly relays a message to the kingdom and soldiers are sent to capture the stranger

Fergie

Then they are most probably looking for us already

Johnson

You found the farm?

Mark

Yes!

Johnson

Then Krumpy must right now be on his way to the western hemisphere, from where messages are relayed to the kingdom

Mark

Western hemisphere? Where is that? And who is Krumpy

Johnson

The western hemisphere is several miles away from here; it takes 3 days to reach there if one travels fast. Krumpy is a dwarf who is the farm custodian. His job is to monitor strangers that get into the trap farm and then notify the palace of their arrival. He's quite lazy so it will probably take him about 5 days to get to the western hemisphere. I think we should intercept him before he arrives there and sends the message

Stingas

Can we set out for the western hemisphere right away?

Amanda

No way! I'm very tired

Johnson

No need to rush things. We'll set out at sunrise tomorrow

They continue eating and drinking.

FADE OUT

FADE IN

It's the next morning and Johnson is in the kitchen making tea from some lemon leaves. Amanda assists him in serving the tea after it is ready.

Johnson

I have lived here for 50 years

Joey

50 years? (*astonished*)

Johnson

Yes, 50 years. I've been here since I was eight years. I live here alone and I'm used to it. My father died in the dungeon

Stingas

So the guard wanted you to escape

Johnson

Not all Gatalinans support the idea of keeping humans captive; a few people believe we deserve freedom

Amanda

What is it about the Bermuda triangle?

Johnson

Long ago, there was a king named Polocas who was a very wicked ruler. He enslaved many Gatalinans, forcefully slept with other people's wives and thus many people didn't like him. After he killed a general's only son, some soldiers plotted against him and he was killed. Since he died, there has been a rift between the kingdom and earth; no one ever came to that boundary for so many years until a time when strangers which are humans were discovered in the kingdom.

The people believed humans were aliens that had come to take over their kingdom so the new king ordered soldiers to capture any stranger found on the land. Many humans were captured, locked up and forced to work as slaves. Many female human slaves have given birth and their children also become slaves, except for those children born of Gatalinan fathers who are allowed to become Gatalinan citizens. These Gatalinan offspring always have blue hair but don't have pointed noses or ears.

Gatalinans are allowed to have sex with any slave they desire. All they have to do is register with the council and then they can take them as wives. Only female human slaves enjoy the benefits of being a wife whereas male slaves work till they die.

Kelly

What a sad story

Johnson

That's the way it is

Stingas

We have no time to waste, let's be on our way

Johnson

We have to first pay a visit to Bolingo, a goddess that was banished from the kingdom for protesting for the freedom of human captives. She likes humans and she'll get us flying brooms that will make our journey easier and faster. She lives after the purest stream and we must cross the stream before noon. If we don't, we will have to wait till tomorrow as the stream dries up at noon.

They all finish their breakfast and start on their way. They walk deep into the forest and after a while they stop to rest.

Fergie

I want to see if I can get an animal to roast. I'm famished

Without waiting for an answer from the others, he walks away, down a valley to the right. After a short walk, he finds a rabbit eating carrots under a tree.

This would be great for lunch (*he smiles*)

He brings out a bow and arrows he had taken from Johnson's cottage and shoots at the rabbit, hitting the target on the first attempt.

Fergie contd

Ah ah ah! This is what I am talking about (*smiling as he walks closer to grab the struck and flailing rabbit*)

As he moves closer, he suddenly begins to hear a cracking sound. He stops for a moment and then he moves a step backward, looking baffled as the rabbit starts to swell up. He watches in amazement as it gets bigger and bigger.

Shit!

He takes another step backward and then he suddenly turns and runs back toward where the others are resting. The rabbit follows him.

Somebody help!! Help me!!! Help!!!

He screams, running as fast as possible.

By now the rabbit has turned into about the size of an elephant with sharp claws protruding from its limbs.

Alerted by Fergie's screams, the others have already gotten up by the time he approaches them.

Fergie

Look! (*he screams and points at the approaching rabbit*)

The others all step backwards, looking in astonishment at the elephant sized rabbit.

I shot at it just once with an arrow

The rabbit is walking toward them slowly, making a growling sound. Stingas and Johnson draw their swords, all the while moving forward slowly. Fergie, Mark, Kelly and Amanda stay behind them looking frightened. The rabbit suddenly swings its right arm towards them in an attempt to hit them with its claws. However, it misses them and topples onto the ground instead. The ground trembles and quakes as the rabbit lands on it and everybody falls to the ground. Almost immediately, they all scramble up, one after the other; and in one accord, they head for the woods, running as fast as possible, with the rabbit after them.

After running for about ten minutes, they come across a cave with a small entrance.

Johnson

To the cave! (*he screams*)

They all scramble into the cave which has an entrance too small for the rabbit to enter through. They hide in the cave watching through the opening as the growling rabbit approaches the cave. Amanda and Kelly are screaming at the top of their voices, with their palms covering their faces. The rabbit stretches its arm into the cave in order to grab one of them but is unable to reach them. Stingas strikes its arm with his sword and the rabbit groans loudly. The rabbit makes a second attempt to grab someone and this time, he gets Joey on the leg.

Joey

Nooooooooooo!!! Help!! (*he cries loudly*)

Johnson, Stingas and Mark immediately grab at Joey's hands, pulling him away from the rabbit's grasp.

Mark

Give us a hand (*yelling at Fergie, Amanda and Kelly*)

Fergie joins them in pulling while Amanda gets a big stone and hits the rabbit on the arm several times.

Mark

Use the sword (*he gestures with his head*)

Amanda grabs Mark's sword and strikes the rabbit on the arm several times. The rabbit finally lets go of Joeys leg, causing them to all fall to the ground as he releases the leg. Fergie quickly grabs his bow and shoots an arrow that hits the rabbit on the neck, weakening it. He shoots several more times until one of the arrows strikes the rabbit in the eye. The rabbit falls to the ground, groaning and rolling over. After some time it stops groaning and rolling over and doesn't move.

Stingas, Mark and Johnson move slowly towards the rabbit.

Kelly

Is it dead?

Stingas

Maybe

Joey

Stay away! I don't think it is dead. That beast is dangerous!

As Stingas and the others approach the rabbit, it rolls over one more time. Stingas immediately sinks his sword into the rabbit's chest and watches as it draw its last breath.

Johnson

I think it is now dead

Stingas

Yes it is

They all heave a sigh of relief.

Johnson

Okay, we must hurry now as we only have a little time before it is noon. Otherwise, we won't be able to cross that stream today

They continue on their journey ………...

Kelly

I'm tired, let's rest for a while

Johnson

No, we must move as fast as possible because it's almost noon

Kelly

I'm too weak to walk (*she falls to her knees*)

Johnson

Don't give up now, we'll soon be there

Mark

Put your arm round my neck (*pulling her up*)

Kelly puts her arm round Mark's neck and they continue on their journey. After a while, they exit the forest and see a mountain ahead of them.

Johnson

That is Mount Cabinas. It's a possessed mountain and spirits of the wild live there

Fergie

Possessed? Spirits?

Johnson

Yes, spirits of the wild. They live on the mountain and they are always blood thirsty. They often come out to hunt for blood so we must be very careful here

Kelly

Everything seems dangerous around here (*looking frightened*)

Johnson

Don't worry, these spirits are blind

Mark

Blind?

Johnson

Yes, they are blind and can't see anything. They can only detect movements or hear sounds when they are passing. If you do not move or make a sound when they pass, then you will be safe as they will just walk by you

Amanda

So how would a person know that they are passing? They are spirits and spirits are invisible ……..

Stingas suddenly stops and cocks his ear to listen. There is a strange sound like an elephant's wail.

Stingas

Wait! (*interrupting Kelly*)……do you hear that?

Fergie

Hear what? You had better quit joking around, Sting

Stingas

This is no joke. Listen!

Mark

Yes, I can hear it. It sounds like an elephant's wail

Johnson

That is no elephant. It's the spirits and they are coming!!

Amanda

Oh my God!

Johnson

Quiet! Come on, follow me (*as he moves swiftly behind a rock*)

Come here!

The others hurriedly rush to join him and they all hide behind the rock.

Fergie

They can't see us so why are we hiding? (*whispering*)

Mark

Shut up Fergie! (*whispering*)

Johnson

Hush! Nobody move, nobody talk!

All of a sudden, there comes a whirlwind; moving from the mountain towards the forest. They remain still and quiet until the whirlwind moves into the forest.

They all sigh out in relief.

Johnson

Now we can continue on our journey

They continue walking and after passing the mountain by, they come to a valley with dragons grazing on the fields.

Joey

Oh my gosh! Dragons!

Johnson

Yes, they are indeed dragons but they are totally harmless. They are an alternate mode of transportation for us apart from flying brooms

Mark

Can we take them for a ride?

Johnson

Yes, it will make our journey go faster

They move closer to the dragons.

Kelly

I'm scared

Johnson

Don't be scared, they are harmless *(as he moves close to one of the dragons and pats it on the head. The dragon bows its head in acknowledgement)*

You see, I told you they are harmless

Take us to the purest stream (*he says to the dragon*)

Dragon

Yes master (*as it lowers its back for them to climb on*)

Everyone but Johnson looks amazed.

Joey

It can talk?

Johnson

Yes they talk

Johnson climbs onto the dragon's back and the others climb on after him, one after the other.

Kelly

Give me a hand please

Mark grabs her hands and pulls her up onto the back of the dragon.

Johnson

Is everybody okay?

Fergie

Yes, I think (*he struggles to gain balance and finally stabilizes himself*)

Johnson

Are we good to go?

Joey

Move it captain! (*grinning widely*)

Johnson

Move it, Droozy

The dragon flaps its wings and flies into the sky.

Fergie

Fly, fly fly….dragon!

Joey

Ooh la la this is fun (*laughing*)

Johnson

You think this is fun? Wait till you get on the flying broom

Fergie

I can't wait! (laughing) Ha ha ha

The dragon picks up speed and begins to fly real fast over deserts, mountains and valleys. By this time, the sun is quite high in the sky.

Johnson

We have very little time left; it's almost noon

Stingas

How far away is the stream?

Johnson

Not too far away, we'll soon be there

After a while, the dragon slows down and descends to the ground.

Joey

Why the hell is it stopping, are we there yet?

Johnson

It can't go beyond this point; the stream is down this hill, we must hurry as we have just a little time left

They all jump off the dragon's back and Johnson pats the dragon on its head.

Dragon

Goodbye master

Johnson

Goodbye Droozy

(*To the others*) Let's hurry up

They all start to run down the hill but Amanda slips and falls. Losing her footing, she rolls down the hill until she finally comes to a stop at the bottom of the hill.

Mark

Holy shit!

They all run down to her side.

Kelly

Are you okay?

Amanda

I'm fine (*panting*)

Mark reaches down to pull her up and Kelly helps her dust the sand off her clothes.

Mark

Are you sure you are okay?

Amanda

I'm fine (*she mutters*)

Johnson

Look, that's the stream down there (*pointing to the stream*)

Let's hurry up, it's almost dried up

By this time, it is noon and the stream is already slowly drying up. There is a canoe parked at the edge of the stream.

Johnson

Come on, let's push the canoe into the stream (*he runs to the canoe with the others running behind him*)

Once we push the canoe into the stream, it won't dry up until we have successfully crossed the stream

Together, they all begin to push the canoe into the stream.

Fergie

It's heavy

Stingas

Just push with all your might

They all push the canoe with all their strength until the canoe slips gently into the stream. By this time, the stream has almost dried up completely. However, as soon as they push the canoe on to the dried streambed, the drying stream is revived. The water slowly returns to the dried-out parts and the stream begins to flow once again.

Johnson

Ooh ooh ooh we made it! We made it! (*laughing*)

They pile themselves into the canoe, laughing and rejoicing.

Kelly

I almost freaked out (*laughing*)

Amanda

Me too, I think I peed in my pants (*everyone laughs*)

The stream water is crystal clear.

Joey

Wow, this is so amazing. The water is crystal clear

Johnson

Yes that's why it is called the purest stream

The canoe sails away by itself without being paddled and moments later, they arrive at the other end of the stream.

Johnson

Here we are. This place is called the Arctic Plains

Joey

Arctic Plains? Why is it called that?

Johnson

Well, you will soon experience it yourself. It's a very cold region and it's always snowing here

Fergie

We don't have coats

Johnson

Don't worry; Bolingo's castle is only a few miles away from here

They move from the stream into the plains where it is snowing steadily. They fold their arms over their chests as they

begin to shiver; and they walk as fast as possible to keep warm.

After they have walked for a short while, they come across a chariot with two white unicorns driving it.

Unicorn 1

Welcome to the Arctic Plains. Her Majesty Bolingo sent us to bring you to her castle

Kelly

Animals here can talk?

Johnson

They are no ordinary animals

They pile into the chariot and it takes off the ground. It flies into the sky swerving left and right around the tall trees and mountains.

Fergie

I love this! I would like to have a chariot like this in Florida (*he laughs*)

The chariots dash about in the sky until they finally arrive at the top of a mountain. On the mountain is a big white castle.

The chariot lands directly in front of the castle's entrance. The castle door opens and standing at the doorway is a woman with very long white hair and dressed in a long, dazzling white robe.

Bolingo

Welcome to my castle

They all climb down from the chariot, still shivering and with arms still folded over their chests.

Bolingo

Come on inside

Johnson

Your Majesty (*he bows*)

Joey

How did you know we were coming?

Bolingo

I am a goddess, I can foresee things (*laughing*)

Joey

Oh! Forgive my ignorance (*he giggles*)

They walk in through the beautifully carved castle doors.

Kelly

This is a beautiful castle

Bolingo

Thank you.

Every part of the castle's interior is white and there are female maids all around, busy at work. As Bolingo leads them up the stairs, Fergie winks at one of the maids who returns it with a smile. Bolingo gives them each a coat and then takes them to the dining table. Three maids come in and serve them food.

Bolingo

I foresee victory in your mission

Fergie

Hopefully, although it seems rather complicated

Bolingo

(*Ignoring Fergie's utterance, she continues*) ……..but you have to stay focused and I will help you out

Fergie

Are you coming with us?

Bolingo

No, I will only give you guides that you must follow

She sips her drink and continues to speak.

The only way back to earth is through a secret basement in the king's palace. The basement is located behind the palace but it can only be unlocked from the king's room. The king wears a bracelet on his left hand and this bracelet is the key to open this basement

Once the bracelet is placed on the symbol that is on the king's wardrobe, the basement will open for a period of forty minutes before it shuts automatically. Whoever makes it into the basement makes it back to earth

Mark

It seems complicated

Bolingo

Yes, it does but don't worry about it. Everything will work out fine if you stay focused and if you all are brave enough

Bolingo contd

Giolas!

A fairy comes into the room through a door behind them

Giolas

Yes, Your Majesty

Bolingo

These humans are going to need your help so you will go with them to Gatalina, to assist them in their mission

Giolas

Yes, Your Majesty

Bolingo

You must stay with them until their mission is over and if anything goes wrong; make sure you send me a message immediately. You know my mirror signals have been cut off from the kingdom

Giolas

Yes, Your Majesty

Bolingo

(*To the humans*) You can spend the night here and take off tomorrow morning. I will give you three flying brooms for your journey. Giolas will take you to my sister, Relingo whom you will stay with

Johnson

We have to catch up with Krumpy; he is probably on his way to the western hemisphere right now

Bolingo

Oh Krumpy (*she pauses and then continues*). Krumpy is still on his way. You will find him on your way tomorrow, as he's yet to arrive at his destination

She concludes speaking and then calls a maid to take them to the room where they would spend the night. The room is enormous, has eight beds and is painted in white.

In the morning, there is a knock on the door.

Joey

Come on in!

A pretty maid opens the door; she is dressed in a silver robe which is just long enough to cover her thighs. She has long black silky hair and she is carrying a bag in her hands.

Maid

Good morning! Her Majesty asked me to give you this clothes to wear and requests that you meet her in the living room as soon as possible

---

Amanda approaches her and collects the bag from her.

Amanda

Thank you; tell her we will be with her in a moment

The maid curtseys and walks out, closing the door behind her. They all dress up in the new clothes; they are dressed in the manner of the Roman Empire, exactly the way the Gatalinans dress.

They walk to the living room where Bolingo is sitting in a big chair. She is dressed in a long white robe with her long white hair resting on her shoulders. Two maids dressed in short silver robes are standing left and right behind her.

Johnson

Good morning Your Majesty (*he bows*)

Bolingo

Good morning to you all

She snaps her fingers and one of the maids standing behind hands her a wand.

I gave you those clothes to wear so that you can disguise and look like Gatalinans

She flicks the wand from left to right several times and suddenly their hair color changes to blue just like that of the Gatalinans.

Joey

W-w-what! (*looking astonished*)

Does this mean our hair will be blue forever?

Bolingo

Not at all, the spell will undo itself when you return to earth or rather when you leave Gatalina

My chariot will take you to the arctic border; from there you will use the flying brooms, which you will find by the door on your way out of the castle. You will head east and stop by the Cannalis Plains where you will find Krumpy. You must hurry because you have limited time. You will find some swords with the brooms; both items are magical, they become invisible when they are not in use and reappear whenever you need them. The swords are very powerful; the magic on them will help you fight more accurately

At the castle entrance, they see five swords, three knives and three flying brooms floating in the air beside the door. Except for Amanda and Kelly, they each take a sword after which the

swords become invisible. Johnson grabs one broom and throws it to Stingas, then throws another to Fergie. As Fergie catches the broom, it twitches. He is frightened and releases it immediately; Mark catches it. Johnson grabs the last one and they all climb into the chariot and wave goodbye at Bolingo who has been watching them from an upstairs window. She waves back in acknowledgement as the chariot flies off into the sky with Giolas flying behind them.

They reach the arctic border and after dropping them off, the unicorns drive the chariot back to the castle.

Johnson

It's time for us to ride on the broom. Don't be scared because you can never fall off a flying broom. It is powered by magic so just believe in its magic

Johnson takes the broom and puts in between his legs. Immediately, the broom rises up into the air lifting Johnson off the ground.

Come on! (*he beckons at the others*)

Joey gets on Johnson's broom; Kelly and Amanda get on another broom with Mark leading while Fergie gets on the third broom with Stingas.

Johnson

You control it with your mind, follow my lead

They all zoom off with Giolas flying ahead of them. They soar in the watery clouds like eagles. After they have traveled a long way, they arrive at the

Cannalis Plains; and as they get off the brooms, the brooms disappear.

Johnson

Here we are, the kingdom of Gatalina is only a few miles from here

Mark

So how do we find Krumpy?

Giolas

We will track him with the sun (*in a tiny voice*)

Stingas

How?

Giolas

Just watch me

Giolas raises his wand towards the sun. The wand sparkles at the top and the sparks point to the direction behind them.

Giolas

This way (*in a tiny voice*)

Giolas floats up in the air ahead of them while they walk from behind. They see a cave and approach the entrance.

Giolas

Krumpy is in here

They enter the cave, which is dark inside. Giolas flicks his wand and it lights up with a glowing white light that brightens up the cave. They walk deep into the cave and see Krumpy sleeping in a corner with his hat covering his face. He is snoring and after moving close to him, Stingas grabs him by the hand, waking him up.

Krumpy

Who are you people? W-w-what do you want from me?

He struggles to free himself from Stingas' grip but Stingas' clasp is too strong for him.

Stingas

Do they already know we are here?

Krumpy

Who? I don't know what you are talking about!

Stingas hits him with a punch to the face.

Stingas

You pretender! Tell me the truth now

Krumpy

I swear I don't know what you are talking about

Giolas flicks his wand; a rope appears from nowhere and binds Krumpy up. As Krumpy struggles with the rope, Stingas carries him on his shoulder and heads towards the entrance of the cave.

Stingas

Let's get out of here; he will confess after I am finished with him

They all follow behind him.

Krumpy

Leave me alone. Let me go (*he cries*)

It is night and they are all seated under a tree. A pile of wood is burning in a fire. Krumpy is hanging upside down from the tree. Stingas has a whip in his hand and is whipping Krumpy.

Stingas

For the last time, before I chop off your head, have you sent a message to the kingdom?

Krumpy

N-n-n-no I am yet to reach the western hemisphere. I was delayed by the dragon that took me on the journey. It fell ill and I couldn't go any further. It escaped last night

Mark

What took you so long to confess?

He hits Krumpy in the face and Krumpy groans.

Mark contd

They must never know we are here. If they do, consider yourself dead

It is midnight and they are all asleep except for Krumpy who is still awake and is struggling with the rope. An eagle lands on the tree.

Krumpy

Night watcher! *(in a whisper)*

The eagle bites through the rope, cutting it off. As Krumpy falls to the ground, the sound almost wakes up Mark. He stirs

and changes his sleeping position but doesn't wake.

Krumpy

Inform the king that there are strangers at the outskirts. Hurry! (*he whispers*)

The eagle flies away and then Krumpy runs away from the tree as fast as he can. A short while later, Mark wakes up and immediately notices that Krumpy has escaped.

Mark

He is gone! (*he yells*)

They all wake up instantly.

Stingas swerves his hand in the air and his sword appears. Mark does the same.

Stingas

The rest of you stay here; Mark and I will go get him

Giolas

I will also go with you

Mark, Giolas and Stingas walk into the plains. Giolas who is flying ahead of them stops suddenly. He flicks his wand and the sparks point left.

Giolas

This way!

They head towards the left and in the distance; they see Krumpy running down the hills.

Mark

There he is! (*shouting*)

Hearing Mark's shout, Krumpy looks back and sees them. He runs faster but suddenly hits his foot on a stone and falls. He rolls down the hill, scrambles up and continues to run while they run after him. He reaches a small hill and climbs it; Mark and Stingas climb after him while Giolas flies to the top of the hill to wait for him.

As Krumpy gets to the top, Giolas flicks his wand and fires a glowing fireball at him. Krumpy dodges the glowing fireball and keeps running. Mark and Stingas also get to the top of the hill, one after the other. Krumpy runs to the other edge of the mountain but he is running too fast and before he realizes it, it is too late to stop and he falls off the edge. He screams aloud as he falls into a pit below the hill. Mark and Stingas stop and watch as he falls off.

Giolas

He is dead!

They return to the camp where the others are waiting.

Kelly

Did you find him?

Mark

Yes, but he died during the pursuit

Stingas

He fell off a mountain into a pit

Mark

I only hope he hadn't yet sent the message before we discovered him

Johnson

We have to get to Gatalina by dawn

The next morning, they set out on their way to the kingdom. As they move across a desert, a swarm of bees unexpectedly comes buzzing around them.

Fergie

Bees!

Giolas

It's a message from Bolingo

Multiple voices simultaneously speak out from the swarm.

Voices

Last night, a night watch eagle from the kingdom rescued Krumpy and he already sent a message through the eagle to the kingdom. The Gatalinan soldiers are now looking for you and you must get to the kingdom as fast as possible because if they see you out here, they will identify you even with your disguised hair. However, once you are in the kingdom they will never be able to identify you so you must hurry as you only have a little time left

The swarm disappears.

GATALINAN KINGDOM

King Mapheononicus, a heavily built man wearing a golden crown to cover his bald head; with his blue beard curving outward from his chin is sitting in the throne room. He is dressed in silver linen with a gold necklace around his

neck, a diamond bracelet on his left wrist and another on his right wrist. The princess, Samake, a young pretty girl with short blue hair and pointed nose and ears is sitting to the left of the king. The king's chiefs are also seated in the throne room. General Speckles, a mean looking figure with a broad chest and a scar across his left cheek walks in and bows to the king.

Speckles

Your majesty, a message came through last night saying that seven strangers have been seen at the outskirts

King

What are you waiting for? Send your soldiers to start searching for them right away

Speckles

Yes, Your Majesty

He bows and leaves the room.

GATALINAN PALACE

General Speckles approaches Lieutenant Krols, a dashing young officer.

Speckles

Order some soldiers out immediately, they must find the seven strangers at the outskirts as soon as possible. Make sure you deliver them alive

Krols

Yes sir!

Lieutenant Krols gives an order to 20 soldiers to set out on the search; each of them mounts a dragon and rides off.

Meanwhile, the humans are back on their flying brooms with Giolas flying behind them. They approach the Gatalinan kingdom border which has a very large gate guarded by ten Gatalinan soldiers. They hide behind a hill some distance away so that the guards will not see them.

Johnson

Here we are at the Gatalinan kingdom and that is the entrance gate over there

Mark

So how do we get in there? There are soldiers at the gate - is there another entrance to the kingdom

Fergie

(Interrupting Mark) Remember we are disguised? We look like them and they will surely let us in

Johnson

Of course we look like them but no Gatalinan is allowed out of the gate except on special duty. Only the soldiers are allowed

Stingas

But we are not soldiers neither do we look like soldiers

Kelly

Then what do we do? (*looking worried*)

Johnson

I don't know, I am confused

Joey

Giolas, why don't you send a message to Bolingo? She might be able to help us out

Giolas

Uhh! I have an idea. There are security fairies, I will go in and act like one then I'll make them all sleep. Then you can quickly get in

Stingas

What if it doesn't work out?

Johnson

We have to be optimistic here, let's hope it works

Stingas

Okay, let's give it a shot

Giolas flies to the entrance gate while the other wait behind the hill. They remain floating on their brooms ready to buzz in as soon as the coast is clear.

Giolas

Hey officers (*as he approaches the guards*)

I have had a long day. I want to return to the city for a nap; my colleagues are on the watch (*smiling*)

Guard

Okay! Don't be too long

The guard turns and signals another guard to open the gate for Giolas. As they both turn their backs to attend to the gate, Giolas flicks his wand and as it sparkles, all of the soldiers abruptly fall to the ground like they have been shot by a tranquilizer. The others are watching the whole scenario from behind the hill. Giolas signals to them to come over but unknown to him, there are three soldiers on the other side of the gate who have not been affected by the spell.

Giolas

Come on! The coast is clear

They all breeze in through the gate on their brooms. As soon as they get in, Giolas dashes behind them.

The three soldiers approach.

Soldier

Hey stop!

They all stop the brooms mid-air and turn around, looking puzzled

Giolas

W-w-we are on a mission to search…..

Soldier

(*Interrupting him*) Liar! There are no citizens on mission at this time

They realize that they are in trouble and so Giolas attempts to flick his wand to make some magic. The soldier is very fast and quickly strikes Giolas' wand off his hands with his sword. Mark and Stingas jump down from their brooms, draw their swords and attack the soldiers. Moments later, Johnson and Joey also draw their swords and join in the fight. As they engage the three soldiers in a sword battle, their swords suddenly become illuminated, transferring to them some kind of energy and confidence that enabled them to conquer all the soldiers.

With the fight over and the three soldiers killed, they all get back on their brooms.

Giolas

We must hurry now before the other soldiers wake up; the spell will be over soon

They breeze away and fade into the air.

After a while, they reach the city center. It looks just like a typical town from the Roman Empire; there are many Gatalinan citizens moving about and they see streets and houses below as they ride through on their brooms. A few people ride on dragons while most people ride on brooms, which are the major means of transportation.

They ride over the market which has food and jewelry on display. The leaves on the trees are purple and there are fairies all over the city. All the citizens have blue hair.

Mark

Why are there so few people riding on dragons?

Johnson

Dragons are more expensive so it is mostly rich people that ride on them

They arrive at an intersection and Giolas who has been leading the way stops abruptly.

Stingas

What is the problem?

Giolas

I am trying to figure out which way we have to head

Amanda

Where exactly are we going to?

Giolas

Relingo's house, of course

He flicks his wand and it glows to the right.

Giolas contd

Oh yes! This way

He turns to the right and almost bumps into a family of four comprising of a father, mother and their two children. The family is riding on a broom with the father steering at the front.

Man

You had better watch where you are going, you little creature!

Giolas ignores him and breezes off. The others fly behind him until they reach another intersection where Giolas stops again.

Fergie

Oh! What again?

Giolas

Traffic! Look (*he points to an oak tree which glows orange*) that is the traffic indicator

Joey

Traffic?   In this ancient kingdom?

Johnson

Sh-sh-sh-sh you had better watch your speech. Someone might be listening and they will know you are a stranger

(*he whispers*)

All of a sudden, a man from behind them yells.

Man

Move it! The traffic is moving

Now the oak tree is glowing white and so they breeze off; along with several other people on brooms and dragons.

They finally arrive at a light-blue colored house at the end of a street.

Giolas

Here is Relingos' house

RELINGO'S HOUSE

As they approach the door, it opens by itself. They all come down from their brooms and walk inside, into a very beautiful living room. Suddenly there's a voice from across the room.

Relingo

You are just in time

They all turn round and see Relingo sitting on a chair across the room.

Johnson

Good day (*he bows*)

Relingo

I welcome you all to my humble abode

All

Thank you (*they bow*)

Relingo

You must all be tired from your long journey; Mantas will show you to your room

A maid shows up.

Mantas

Please come with me

They follow her.

FADE OUT

FADE IN

They are all eating at the dining table with Relingo.

Relingo

I got a message from Bolingo that you would be coming and you have come at the right time as tonight is the annual festival of Shirk

Kelly

Shirk?

Relingo

Yes it's a god spirit that everybody in this kingdom worships. Our uncle , the former king, was a wicked man and he started the idea when he was alive. People have continued the tradition even though he is dead. They sacrifice three human captives to the god and after the sacrifice has been accepted, they celebrate with a wild party

Fergie

Must we attend the festival?

Relingo

Everybody in the kingdom must attend; if you don't, they will suspect you are strangers. Besides, it is necessary for your mission that you attend

Stingas

They sacrifice human captives? That is brutality

Relingo

You must keep your calm during that time and not arouse suspicions. Lest I forget, the guards you killed at the gates have been found by Lieutenant Krols and his men and they now suspect that you lot are in the kingdom

Mark

Oh, so what do we do now?

Relingo

(*She smiles*) ….. Not to worry, I wiped the events off the memory of those soldiers that slept off. The dead soldiers have been buried and new guards have been appointed to the border gates

Johnson

Wow, thank you so much (*looking relieved*)

GATALINAN SQUARE

Thousands of Gatalinans are gathered at the square to witness the festival. The king is sitting on his throne and Princess Samake is sitting on the left hand side of the king. The king's chiefs are also seated and the crowd is gathered in a semi-circle around the podium where the king and his chiefs are seated. Three raised platforms are in the middle.

The crew arrives at the venue with Relingo.

Relingo

According to the custom, I have to be seated with the king's chiefs

Joey

We are going to be all by ourselves?

Relingo

Don't worry; I will be with you as soon as the festival is over

Relingo leaves them and heads for the podium.

King

Distinguished citizens of the great Gatalinan kingdom - the 142nd annual festival of Shirk is about to begin

The crowd claps and cheers him on.

King contd

The festival will begin with the traditional sacrifice …. now let the festival begin

The crowd roars in agreement.

Then there is grave silence as the chief priest Frix, a grizzled lean old man steps forward and chants in an ancient tongue. General Speckles comes

forward with three bound human captives. Stingas is looking furious and Johnson signals to him to be calm.

The three human captives are each laid on the three raised platforms by two guards. As Frix finishes his chanting, everywhere is quiet and for a couple of seconds nothing happens. The captives look tensed up but the king and his chiefs look baffled. All of a sudden, there is lightning from the river-like sky followed by a peal of thunder. Bubbles emerge from the river-like sky and a group of singers standing to the side, all dressed in an attire of white linen with a red suede jacket, start to sing:

BOMBAY KARABOM BOM BAYER,
BOMBAY KARABOM BOM BAYER

As they sing, a very big bat about the size of a dinosaur emerges from the sky and eats up the human captives one after the other. After eating the last captive, the bat disappears and the whole crowd roars with joy and jubilation. The singers stop singing.

Frix

The sacrifice has been accepted

King

Let the celebration begin (*with a beaming smile*)

The crowd roars in agreement and the festival begins with much singing and dancing amongst the crowd.

After a while of celebration, the celebration host Mafiosi comes forward.

Mafiosi

It is time for the special dance; therefore let all interested single ladies come forward

Thirteen young ladies go forward, (Mafiosi counts) 1-2-3-4……12-13

Mafiosi

Thirteen is not a good number, we need one more lady

He waits for a while, but nobody else goes forward.

Amanda

I want to go (*she whispers*)

Joey

Are you out of your mind? You are not a Gatalinan

Johnson

Let her go if she really wants to, it is only a contest

Mark

What do you think, Giolas?

Giolas

Let her, if she wants

Amanda

I just want to have fun, that's all

The crowd roars as she walks out to the front and as she approaches the podium, she glances at Relingo, who returns a thin smile.

Mafiosi

Before the contest begins, let me formally announce that the winner of this contest will have the honor of dining with the royal family tonight. The criterion for winning is the endurance of the contestants so the last woman standing wins

Let the contest begin!

The crowd is ecstatic.

The royal band begins to play with drums, trumpet and harps, producing a

fast tune. The fourteen contestants dance for several minutes until some of them begin to get tired. They are evicted one after the other as their fatigue is detected. After a while, there are only three contestants left, including Amanda. During the dance, the king can be seen looking lustfully at Amanda's shapely figure.

After struggling with her endurance for a couple of minutes, Amanda finally tires out and gets evicted. As soon as she is evicted, the king calls General Speckles to his side and whispers to his ear.

General Speckles then goes to whisper into a guard's ear.

As Amanda goes back into the crowd, the guard goes after her.

Soldier

Hey miss!

Amanda is frightened.

Amanda

W-w-what? (*she stutters*)

Soldier

Don't be scared Miss, the king has asked to see you and you might be getting a royal treatment tonight (*he winks*)

Stingas

(*Stingas interrupts*) Stay away from her, she is my sister!

Soldier

Hey, no harm meant, the king wants your sister and if she is interested, she should come to the palace after the festival to dine with the royal family…and your name is?

Amanda

Amanda!

Soldier

Very well

The soldier walks away.

FADE OUT

FADE IN

The festival is over and Relingo rejoins the crew.

Johnson

The king invited Amanda to join the royal family for supper. What do you think Relingo?

Relingo

That is great, what a stroke of luck!

Stingas

What do you mean?

Relingo

It means that king has some romantic interest in Amanda. That will help you to get closer to the bracelet and near the end of your mission.

Johnson

Oh! I see. That is quite true

Amanda

I won't go, never!

Fergie

Why? You can't do that to us, you know our fate now depends on you

Amanda

I am scared. What if they discover I am not a Gatalinan? They will feed me to that monster at the next festival

Relingo

Don't worry, I will keep watch over you and I will do my utmost to protect you

Amanda

Okay, I will go

It is evening; Amanda, Mark and Stingas arrive at the palace entrance and approach the two soldiers on guard.

Soldier

How may I help you?

Mark

We have an invitation from the king

Soldiers

The king will never invite you low class people to the palace *(laughing)*

General Speckles comes out through a door.

Speckles

Your name?

Amanda

Amanda!

Speckles

Let her in

Amanda

Thank you

As she walks in through the gate, Mark and Stingas try to follow her and are stopped by the soldiers.

Soldier

Hey stop! Not you two

Speckles

Who are they?

Amanda

They are my brothers

Speckles

I am afraid they will have to wait in the lobby unless the king says otherwise

In the royal dining room; the king, the princess and five of the king's chiefs are sitting. Speckles approaches the king.

Speckles

She is here

King

Great! Bring her in

Speckles escorts Amanda into the dining room.

King

Welcome! Have a seat (pointing to a vacant chair on his right hand side)

Amanda is visibly uncomfortable.

King

Relax, you are home. Before we begin our dinner, I would like to seize this opportunity to introduce my new queen, Queen Amanda

Amanda is astonished and is about to say something when she suddenly hears a voice whispering into her ear; a voice only she can hear.

Voice

Play along with the king; show interest and arouse no suspicions

Amanda pulls herself together.

Amanda

The pleasure is mine, your majesty. However, before any further introduction, I would like my brothers to be present here

King

(*Smiling*) that's no problem at all….where are they?

Amanda

In the outer lobby

King

Get them in, Speckles

Speckles

Yes, your majesty!

Speckles brings Mark and Stingas in to the king.

King

I am pleased to meet you; join us for dinner

They both take their seats and join in the dinner.

FADE OUT

FADE IN

The next morning, standing on the palace balcony, the king introduces Amanda to the Gatalinan people as his new queen. Fergie, Kelly and Giolas are present in the crowd.

After the ceremony Amanda is alone with the king in their room.

Amanda

Thank you for letting my brothers stay in the palace with me. They are all I've had since we lost our parents a long time ago

King

What more could I possibly do for my queen? If there is anything else you desire, don't hesitate to ask

Amanda

You are so kind

King

I will do my utmost to satisfy my beloved queen

Amanda

I desire to bring in my servants to come and work for me here at the palace

King

Uh, not a bad idea, but there are numerous servants here in the palace

Amanda

Yes, that is true but you should understand that they have been working with me for a long time and I am used to them

King

Okay, whatever my queen desires; Krols will send for them as soon as possible

Amanda

Thank you, your majesty

Krols arrives with two palace guards and knocks on Relingo's door, which then opens by itself. Joey and Fergie are sitting in the living room and are frightened as the soldiers walk in.

Krols

You must be Joey? (*as he turns to Joey*)

Joey

What do you want? (*stuttering*)

Krols

You and the others are wanted in the palace by order of the king

Fergie

What did we do wrong? (*looks terrified*)

Krols

The queen wants you to continue working for her at the palace

Fergie

Oh, with all pleasure (*giggles, looking relieved*)

Joey

Let me inform the others

Krols

Make it snappy, I don't have much time

Joey runs into the inner room to inform the others.

Joey

Amanda has requested that we come to the palace to work for her

Giolas

Great! Just exactly as we want it to be

Joey

Relingo, do they know this is your house?

Relingo

No, not at all, they only know about my late father's house. (*Whispering*) - Now that your mission is about to really begin, you must be very careful and most importantly you must all stay focused

Krols

We should be on our way by now (*yelling from the living room*)

Relingo

You must go now; they must not know I am here, no one knows I stay here

Kelly

Alright …… Thank you so much

Fergie, Joey, Johnson and Kelly leave with Krols and the guards to the palace.

The king is sitting on his throne in the throne room with Amanda sitting to his right and Princess Samake to his left when Krols enters with Fergie, Joey, Johnson and Kelly

Krols

Here they are, your majesty (*he bows*)

King

Very well. Are you pleased, my beloved queen?

Amanda

Yes, your majesty (*with a beaming smile*)

Amanda contd

Lieutenant Krols

Krols

Yes, queen

Amanda

The three men will be working as cleaners while the lady will join in the kitchen; please assign them as appropriate

Krols

Right away, queen

PALACE CORRIDOR (NIGHT)

Later that night, Stingas and Mark meet with the others along a corridor.

Mark

Good to see you all again but we must be careful not to act like we are friends as we must leave no room for suspicion

Johnson

Yes, and we must stay focused …….. no one must get carried away by the luxuries of the palace

Stingas

Our fate now depends on Amanda; I hope she is strong enough to handle this

Johnson

She will, let's be optimistic

The next morning, Mark and Stingas are walking along a passageway in the palace when they see about a hundred human captives being marched along by two soldiers, each soldier holding a

horse whip. The human captives are chained together on their legs.

Soldier

Move it! (*he whips the captives at random*)

Mark is moved by pity but quickly gathers himself together so as not to arouse any suspicions.

Stingas

Let us follow them to see where they are being taken to (*whispering to Mark*)

Mark

Alright

They follow the soldiers, trying to look inconspicuous. The captives are led out of the palace through a wide gate on to a large wheat field. There are about eight hundred captives already working; some are harvesting wheat while some are breaking rocks. There are lots of soldiers stationed around the perimeter of the field to supervise and whip the captives as they work.

Stingas

This is bullshit!

Mark

There has to be an end to this

Stingas

We need to rescue all human captives as part of our mission

Mark

I hope opportunity and time will allow us to do so

It is evening as Stingas wanders around the palace and finds the dungeon where the human captives are kept. There are lots of soldiers on guard but a particular heavy-built soldier with a peacock feather in his cap is standing at the doorway to the dungeon. The captives are just being marched backed to the dungeon and the heavy built soldier reaches for a big key hanging on his belt and opens the dungeon door. From behind the big statue where Stingas is hiding, he can see into the dungeon which is large enough to contain about a thousand captives. As the captives move into the dungeon, the soldiers whips them randomly, eliciting groans of pain. There are more male captives than females.

PALACE THRONE ROOM

General Speckles approaches the king, with six wealthy looking Gatalinan men following one step behind him.

Speckles

Your majesty, six merchants are here to see you. They have requested for human wives and await your final consent

King

You have my consent! Bring some female captives and let them choose the ones they want

Speckles

Yes your majesty

Moments later, twenty female captives are brought to the throne room. The six merchants walk around to inspect them and each of them select a female of his choice.

King

Our suitors seem to be pleased with their choices

Merchants

Yes, Your Majesty (they chorus in unison)

King

Have them sign the register before they go away with their new wives or concubines, as the case may be

He laughs and the merchants also laugh.

The rest of the female captives are returned to the dungeon.

PALACE LIVING ROOM (DAY)

Princess Samake and her friend Sonetta are sitting in the living room; Fergie and Joey are on the other end of the room cleaning up.

Samake

I think that guy is cute

Sonetta

Which guy?

Samake

The one with the long hair (*pointing at Fergie*)

Sonetta

Hmm, whatever

Samake

I like him

Sonetta

What! Are you crazy? Don't tell me you are falling in love with an ordinary servant. Do you remember that you are a princess?

Samake

What does it matter?

The princess smiles at Fergie from the distance as he glances toward their direction. Fergie smiles back as he picks up the trash can and leaves the room with Joey.

Fergie

Did you see that? (*as they walk along a passageway*)

Joey

See what?

Fergie

The princess was smiling at me

Joey

She was probably sharing a joke with her friend

Fergie

No, no …. I could see the passion in her eyes

Joey

Cut out the crap, are you trying to say that she likes you?

Fergie

I think so

Joey

You are full of fantasies (*chuckles*)

PALACE BACKYARD

Johnson is at the palace backyard feeding the royal dragons when Giolas appears to him.

Giolas

You have to get an urgent message across to Amanda. The king is going to drink a lot of wine tonight, so she has to use the opportunity to try to get the bracelet. All of you must be alert and ready by the basement

Johnson

But why don't you appear to her and tell her this yourself? I am not allowed to see her or even talk to her

Giolas

There is a charm in the palace that opposes the magic of fairies; I can only communicate with you outside the palace. The king will rip off my head if I am caught so I have to go now. Don't fail to tell Amanda, please do as I say

Giolas disappears. Johnson goes to the palace kitchen and signals to Kelly who is baking with some other women. She gets the signal.

PALACE KITCHEN

Kelly

Excuse me please (*as she leaves the kitchen*)

Johnson and Kelly are alone in the corridor; Johnson looks to the right and

to the left to make sure no one is coming.

Johnson

There is a message from Giolas that must be delivered to Amanda as soon as possible; you are the only one that can get close enough to Amanda.

KING'S BEDROOM

Amanda is alone in the royal bedroom when there is a knock on the door.

Amanda

Come on in!

Kelly enters the room with a tray in her hand and serves lemon tea to the queen.

Kelly

Are you alone? (*she whispers as she pours the tea into the cup*)

Amanda

Yes, any message?

Kelly

The king is going to be drinking a lot of wine tonight and you are to make sure he gets drunk so you can get the bracelet. You know what you must do after that; we will be waiting for you at the southern door of the palace. Try to be as fast as possible - you know the basement will only be open for forty minutes

Amanda

I am scared (*grabs Kelly by the hand*)

Kelly

I understand, but you have to be strong and brave as our fate depends on it

There is a clicking sound at the door as it opens and the king walks in. Kelly gets up quickly and picks up the tray.

Kelly

Your Majesty, will that be enough?

Amanda

Yes, thank you

Kelly walks out quickly and curtseys to the king as she exits the door and closes it behind her. The king notices that Amanda is trembling.

King

You are trembling, my queen. Are you alright?

Amanda

I am fine, just feeling a little cold, that's why I requested for some tea

King

Very well my queen (*not looking too convinced*)

Amanda sips her tea, she looks very tensed up.

FADE OUT

FADE IN

PALACE BACKYARD

Johnson, Joey, Mark and Stingas are at the palace backyard where the royal dragons are kept.

Stingas

I think we should be able to rescue the rest of the human captives, so that they can escape with us

Johnson

We only have a little time to escape; besides how do we do get them out of the dungeon?

Mark

The dungeon is heavily guarded and even if we try, we can't fight all the guards in this palace before time runs out and the basement door closes. Our mission will fail and you know what that means

Joey

We will be trapped here forever

Johnson

And one day we might be discovered too and thrown into the dungeon as captives

Stingas

There must be a way

Joey

Perhaps we should get a message across to some of the captives about the secret basement; I think that's the best we can do

AT THE PALACE BATH POOL

The princess and her friend Sonetta are bathing in the pool of water. Two palace maids are with them; one is bathing the princess while the second is bathing Sonetta.

Princess

Do you know any of the palace servants by the name Fergie? (*speaking to the maid bathing her*)

Maid

Yes Princess; he is a cleaner in the palace

Princess

I demand to see him at the garden immediately after my bath

Maid

Yes, princess

Sonetta

I guess you are not going to give up on this guy

Princess

I have got a soft spot for him (*smiling as she sips her wine*)

PALACE GARDEN (NIGHT)

It is evening; the princess is waiting for Fergie at the palace garden. Fergie shows up with a maid.

Maid

Princess, here he is, as you requested

Princess

Thank you, you may leave us alone

The princess looks up at Fergie from where she is sitting.

Princess

You must be surprised

Fergie

As matter of fact, not really

Princess

What do you mean?

Fergie

Forgive me princess, but I have dreamt about this moment and I have been hoping for this day

Princess

I would like to see you often. You are such a handsome looking man (*she stands up and caresses Fergies's chin*) …. And you are too cute to be a servant

Fergie

Thanks for the compliment. Although it is well known that princesses are always beautiful, however, I think that your beauty is exceptional. I can't resist your beauty anytime I set my eyes on you

The princess places her index finger on Fergie's lips.

Princess

Shshshshshsh!

The princess leans to kiss Fergie and they kiss passionately. The princess pulls away after a while.

Princess

I have to go now; nobody in the palace must ever find out about us

Fergie

Sure, see you soon, my princess

The princess departs.

THRONE ROOM

The king is sitting with his chiefs and well-wishers. Amanda is also with them and they are all drinking wine, eating meat, making merry and chatting with each other.

King

It is good to make merry at times, isn't it my queen?

Amanda

Yes, your majesty (*faking a smile*)

After a while the king is obviously getting drunk. Amanda is looking more tensed; she holds her cup of wine but doesn't drink from it.

King

More wine, please

A short while later, Kelly and three other maids walk in with more wine. Kelly quickly walks up to serve the king while the other maids serve the guest. As

Kelly pours wine into the king's goblet, she winks at Amanda who nods her head in agreement. As Kelly finishes serving, she swiftly runs out to drop the tray at the kitchen and hurries out. One of the maids in the kitchen looks after her suspiciously as she runs out of the kitchen.

PALACE KITCHEN

Maid 1

That maid has been acting strange lately

Maid 2

I noticed too

THRONE ROOM (NIGHT)

The king has become very drunk.

Amanda

Please excuse me distinguished guests, I need to take my king inside now; he needs some rest

She holds the king by the hand and they both walk away, with the king leaning on her.

King

See you soon my friends (*drunkenly*)

Amanda gets the king into the room, he drops on the bed and falls into a deep sleep, snoring.

KING'S BEDROOM (NIGHT)

Amanda

This is the time (*from her thoughts*)

She is developing cold feet and is pacing up and down the room. Confused and nervous, she takes another glance at the bracelet on the king's left hand and moves closer. She slowly holds the king's left hand and raises it up. She drops it but the king does not move.

Amanda

If I am caught I will be the next sacrifice for that beast (*from her thoughts*)

She summons up courage and takes the king's hand yet again. She examines the bracelet to locate where to undo it. She finds the clasp and removes the bracelet with a click. The diamonds on the bracelet glitter as she holds up the bracelet. She takes another look at the king and seeing that he is still in deep sleep, she gets up quickly and makes for the door. As she approaches the door and grabs the handle to open it, she hears the king's voice.

King

And where do you think you are going with that bracelet?

Amanda gasps and turns around. To her greatest surprise, the king is sitting on the bed, fully awake.

King contd

Do you think you can play pranks on a king like me?

Amanda

N-n-no, I was only taking a look at it

King

You liar! You are going to be killed for that. Tonight!

Amanda

No, my lord, please have mercy! (*she falls on her knees crying*)

FADE IN

FADE IN

Amanda is on the bed, sitting by the king and gazing at the diamond bracelet on the king's left hand. As she looks around, she realizes that she had only been imagining things.

Amanda

I just have to take this risk (*from her thoughts*)

She takes the king's left hand and raises it up as she attempts to undo the bracelet….

PALACE SOUTHERN DOOR

The others are already waiting at the southern door.

Joey

What could be keeping her so long?

Fergie

Maybe she has been caught

Joey

Oh shut up! Be optimistic for once

Fergie

We have to be realistic; she is taking too long

Johnson

It's true, maybe something went wrong

Kelly

I am scared; I hope she is still safe

Johnson

Come with me, Mark; let's stay outside because a message might come from Giolas

---

ROYAL BEDROOM

The king suddenly wakes up. Amanda is frightened and quickly let go of the king's hand. The king is still drowsy and his vision is blurry.

King

What are you doing?

Amanda

Oh! I was just trying to make sure you are having a good rest, your majesty (*smiling*)

King

By gazing on my bracelet?

Amanda

I was just admiring it

The king gets up and looks into Amanda's eyes.

King

I hope you were not up to anything funny (*he struggles to gain balance as he stands up*)

The king walks out of the room, still looking drowsy. Amanda is left alone in the room. Looking frightened and tensed up, she buries her face in her palms.

Amanda

I screwed up

PALACE BACKYARD

Johnson and Mark arrive outside the palace backyard and immediately Giolas appears.

Johnson

Uh! I knew you were going to come. Please, what is happening to Amanda?

Giolas

I am sorry to say that Amanda was unable to get the bracelet. She almost got it but the king woke up and caught her. She denied doing anything wrong but the king is now suspicious

Johnson

What do we do now?

Giolas

I will get a message from Relingo as soon as possible; she will know what to do in order to ensure your safety

PALACE THRONE ROOM

The king rushes into the throne room and sits on the throne, still feeling drowsy. All the guests are gone.

King

I need to see Speckles immediately

Guard

Yes, Your Majesty

Moments later, Speckles enters the throne room.

Speckles

Your majesty (*he bows*)

King

I need to see the chief priest, Frix, immediately!

Speckles

Right away, Your Majesty

Chief Priest Frix enters the throne room.

King

Leave us alone guards, this is confidential

Frix

You sent for me, your majesty

King

Yes! I am baffled, something happened

Frix

What could it be, your majesty?

King

I'm suspicious of Amanda, my queen. I woke up from sleep only to find her gazing at my bracelet

Frix

Ooh! That's ridiculous

King

Oh yes, she told me she was only admiring it but I am not fully convinced. Someone might be up to something here. I want you to find out and get to the root of this matter

BOLINGO'S CASTLE (NIGHT)

Bolingo is standing in front of a mirror, chanting in an ancient tongue, with her wand in her hand. Suddenly the palace scene appears on the mirror, showing chief priest Frix chanting with his palms facing upward and a ray of white light falling on his palms.

Bolingo points her wand at the mirror; blue colored lightning flash comes out of her wand and through the mirror. The blue colored lightning interrupts the white rays falling on Frix's palms and the white rays turn blue.

Bolingo heaves a sigh of relief.

Bolingo

Done! (*smiling*)

PALACE THRONE ROOM

Frix finishes his enchantment and smiles.

King

What are you smiling about?

Frix

You have nothing to worry about; your queen was just being inquisitive. All is well

King

Are you sure?

Frix

Would you ever doubt the chief priest of the great Gatalinan kingdom?

King

Forgive my doubts; in that case, I will have to apologize to my beloved queen

---

Frix nods his head.

KING'S BEDROOM

Amanda is on in the terrace; she is scared to think of what the king's decision might be. There is a clicking sound as the door opens and the king walks in. He looks around the room and is surprised not to see Amanda in the room.

King

Amanda! (*he beckons*)

Amanda gets up from the couch on the terrace. She is very frightened; she has her hands across her chest and is gasping as she tries to control her breath.

King contd

Where are you?

The king walks toward the terrace. Amanda is in a corner panting.

King

Why are you hiding from me? I'm not going to harm you. It's alright; I understand that you were only curious about the bracelet

The king pulls her to him and kisses her on the forehead; Amanda shows relief.

PALACE LIVING ROOM

It is the next morning; Johnson and Joey are mopping the floor.

Joey

Now that Amanda's mission has failed, what do we do?

Johnson

I'm sure Giolas will bring a message soon

A swarm of bees suddenly buzzes in front of them and they hear multiple voices coming from the swarm.

Voices

Giolas has a message for you, come outside

Johnson

I told you (*to Joey*)

Johnson and Joey carry their mopping buckets with them and walk out to the backyard. Giolas appears to them immediately.

PALACE BACKYARD

Giolas

Bolingo has taken care of the king's suspicions but now, the success of your mission depends on Fergie

Joey

Fergie? That nitwit?

Johnson

Fergie is a coward!

Giolas

The princess is in love with Fergie. The princess has a bracelet that looks exactly like the king's own. She must exchange it for the king's before he leaves on a long journey in three days. This will be your last chance to escape. Most of the soldiers will be going with him and there will be just a few soldiers left in the palace, which will make your mission easier. Remember you have just three days …… three days

Giolas disappears.

PALACE GARDEN

Later that night, the crew is outside under a tree.

Fergie

This is ridiculous! She will most probably tell her father and we will all get killed

Johnson

You must believe in Bolingo, she gave these instructions. Remember that this is our last chance and if we don't use this opportunity, we might be trapped here forever

Fergie

She gave Amanda instructions too and that plan failed

Mark

At least she took care of the situation and we are still safe. Otherwise we would all be in that dungeon by now

Joey

Fergie, remember your carelessness got us into this mess and now you have get us out! (*glaring at Fergie*)

PALACE PASSAGEWAY (DAY)

Fergie is having breakfast with the other servants when a maid walks up to him and whispers into his ears.

Maid

The princess wants to see you in the garden

Fergie gets to the garden and but does not see the princess. He looks around trying to find the princess while she quietly sneaks out of a flowerbed behind Fergie and creeps to his back. She swiftly covers his eyes with her palms;

Fergie turns around immediately and removes her hands.

Fergie

Oh! You frightened me

Samake

I just wanted to surprise you

They kiss each other passionately. The princess pulls away and drags him to a secluded area in the garden where they are shielded from prying eyes and they resume kissing passionately. The passion builds up between them and they make love. After they are done, they lay side by side on the grass, gazing at the watery sky.

Fergie

Do you truly love me, princess?

Princess

Yes of course! Do you have any doubts?

Fergie

Well, not at all, I just want to be reassured

Princess

I love you so much

She tries to kiss Fergie but Fergie stops her.

Fergie

Wait!

Princess

What's wrong?

Fergie

There is something I need to tell you (*sitting upright*)

Princess

What is it?

Fergie

I hope you will still love me after if I tell you (*looking tensed and breathing heavily*)

Princess

You are freaking me out. Say it, I will always love you

Fergie

Are you sure?

Princess

Yes! I'm sure

Fergie

Promise to tell no one

Princess

I promise

Fergie

Alright, the truth about me is this. I am not a Gatalinan, I am human

Princess

You must be crazy!

Fergie

I know it's hard to believe, but it's true

Princess

(*Looking baffled*) but your hair?

Fergie

I am disguised

Princess

Bolingo?

Fergie

How did you know?

Princess

She is the only one that can do that

But I'm confused. This sounds crazy, this must be a dream

Princess Samake cries out and runs into the palace. Fergie runs after her but does not catch up with her.

Fergie

Wait! Please wait!

The princess dashes into the palace.

Later in the night, Fergie reports what happened to the crew.

Fergie

Oh my God! What have I done?

Johnson

Relax …… let's wait for the outcome

Mark

I trust Bolingo will handle this and we will be safe

Kelly

What if it doesn't work out this time?

Mark

We have to keep our heads together

PRINCESS SAMAKE'S ROOM

The princess is sitting on the floor in a corner of the room, looking worried. Her friend, Sonetta walks in.

Sonetta

What's wrong?

Princess

Nothing

Sonetta

You can't sit there looking worried and tell me nothing is wrong with you

Princess

Nothing is wrong with me. All I want is some privacy, please leave me alone

Sonetta

Alright, whatever, I just hope that servant lover of yours is not behind this (*as she walks out of the room*)

PALACE GARDEN

Princess Samake and Fergie meet at the garden.

Princess

What exactly do you want me to do?

Fergie

My friends and I want to return to earth. To do so, we have to swap your bracelet with the king's own. I know it sounds difficult but you are the only one that can do it. If your father finds out, he will have no choice but to forgive you as you are his only daughter. If anyone else tries it, that person will be killed

The princess sobs.

Princess

That's not possible

Fergie

I know it will be painful for you as much as it will be painful for me, but I just have to return to earth. It is where I belong and this is where you belong. Besides it's time to face the truth. We can never be together; you are a princess and you can't marry a mere servant, not to talk of a human. Please do this in memory of the love we have shared

Princess

What if I am caught in the process?

Fergie

You will not be caught. Amanda will make the swap. Please, we have just 2 days remaining before the king leaves

PALACE ENTRANCE

General Speckles is standing outside. A chariot with two dragons at the head is parked outside the palace. Hundreds of soldiers are behind the chariot, each of the soldiers is mounted on a dragon.

Speckles

I hope everything is set?

Krols

Yes General, we are good to go

Speckles

Very well, now we await the king

PRINCESS SAMAKE'S ROOM

Amanda knocks on Princess Samake's door. The princess opens the door and looks left and right down the hallway to make sure no one is coming.

Amanda

It is time

The princess brings out her diamond bracelet and gives it to Amanda who collects it. As Amanda turns around to leave, the princess holds her back and looks into her eyes.

Princess

I am doing this for Fergie and not for you

Amanda

Thank you

KING'S BEDROOM

Amanda runs back to the king's bedroom. The king is in the bath pool. Amanda enters the bath pool room holding the bracelet with her hands behind her back.

Amanda

Can I have the pleasure of joining my beloved king in the pool before he embarks on his long journey (*smiling?*)

King

Sure, the pleasure is mine (*with a beaming smile*)

Amanda strips off her clothing and hides the bracelet in her bathrobe. She holds the robe, letting it trail behind her. As she steps into the pool, she lets the robe drop at the edge of the pool. She begins to kiss the king passionately and he responds. He reaches out to caress Amanda's back but she resists.

King

What's wrong?

Amanda

Forgive me, my lord. Something on your hand is scratching my skin and hurting me

The king is impatient and can't wait to continue with the lovemaking.

King

Oh! It must be my bracelets.

He removes the two bracelets; the one on his left wrist as well as the one on his right wrist. Amanda watches him carefully as he removes them in order to avoid mixing up the two bracelets later. The king places the two bracelets at the edge of the pool, close to Amanda's robe.

King contd

Now, shall we continue?

Amanda

Oh yes!

The king grabs her and begins to kiss her passionately. As they kiss, Amanda stealthily maneuvers the king's back to the bracelets and her robe. The king kisses Amanda on her neck and she moans. She moves the king to the edge of the pool; close enough to get her hand on her robe and bracelets. She then stretches her hands from behind the king but she is unable to grasp the bracelets so she leans forward, pressing her breasts towards the king who is now lost in ecstasy.

She makes a second attempt and slowly grabs her robe with her left hand and brings out Princess Samake's bracelet. As she attempts to make the swap, she pauses for a second, confused as to which bracelet had been on the king's left hand. After a few seconds, she shrugs, picks up one and swiftly slips it into her robe.

She replaces the king's bracelet with Princess Samake's and as soon as she is done, she breathes out in relief. She begins to respond more passionately to the king's caresses and they make love in the pool.

Amanda

You will have to hurry now; everyone is waiting for you

King

That's right

Amanda gets out of the pool, carefully picks up her robe in a bunch, preventing the bracelet from falling out and walks into the bedroom.

The king starts dressing up; after wearing his clothes, he picks up the bracelets and wears one on each wrist.

PALACE ENTRANCE

The king comes out through the palace entrance, accompanied by Amanda and the princess. Two guards are behind them.

King

Are we set to leave?

Speckles

Yes, your majesty (*bowing*)

King

Lieutenant Krols, you will be in charge of the palace security as Speckles will be going with me on the journey

Krols

Yes, Your Majesty

The king gets into the carriage and waves goodbye to Amanda and Princess Samake. General Speckles gets on the dragon in front of the king's carriage and they all go sailing into the air.

Amanda hurries back to the bedroom, gets dressed in a short gown and brings out the bracelet from under the pillow where she had hidden it.

PALACE LOBBY

Johnson walks up to Joey.

Johnson

It's time, Mark and Stingas are waiting behind the palace (*whispering*)

PALACE KITCHEN

Amanda walks to the kitchen and signals Kelly who casually picks up a potato and chews on it as she walks out the kitchen door.

PALACE BACKYARD

Mark and Stingas are already waiting; Johnson and Joey arrive

Johnson

Where is Fergie?

Mark

He went to give the princess a last kiss; just to say thank you

Johnson nods his head, and then Kelly arrives.

Kelly

I am nervous, I hope nothing goes wrong

Mark draws her to him.

Mark

Don't worry, it will be fine

Giolas appears suddenly.

Giolas

My mission with you is now complete and I must go

Joey

Any word from Bolingo or Relingo?

Giolas

They foresee success

Stingas

That's good news

Johnson

Thank you so much Giolas

Giolas

The pleasure is mine and I wish you all good luck. Goodbye (*as he flicks his wand and disappears*)

Crew

Goodbye (*all waving to him*)

Giolas disappears.

PALACE GARDEN

Fergie is with the princess at the garden.

Fergie

Thank you so much, I will forever appreciate you

They kiss each other. Fergie removes his necklace and gives it to Princess Samake.

Fergie contd

Use this to remember me by; know that my friends and I will forever remember you

Princess

I love you (*sobbing*)

Fergie

I love you too, my princess. I must go now as my friends will be waiting for me

Fergie kisses Princess Samake on the forehead and leaves.

PALACE BACKYARD

Fergie joins the rest of the crew.

Johnson

Amanda will be unlocking the basement anytime from now

Stingas

As there are just a few soldiers in the palace, we should be able to rescue the other human captives

Joey

No Stingas, we won't have enough time to do so and it might ruin the whole plan

Mark

I think Stingas is right, let's try to rescue them

Stingas

I have a plan. Mark and I will go to the dungeon while the rest of you wait here for us. There are only two soldiers guiding the dungeon. We will take them down, and get the key from the third guard who stands across from the dungeon

Johnson

I'll go with you

Amanda is back in the royal bedroom. She locks the door behind her and takes a deep breath. She then brings out the bracelet and walks towards the

wardrobe. Staring at the symbol on the wardrobe, she raises the bracelet and slowly places it on the symbol. The bracelet is immediately magnetized by the symbol but nothing happens. Thinking that she must have taken the wrong bracelet, Amanda is immediately saddened and is about to burst into tears when suddenly, the symbol becomes illuminated. She gasps then smiles in relief and takes a step backwards.

Amanda

It worked! (*softly*)

Amanda hurries out of the bedroom. Locking the door behind her with the key, she runs towards the southern door to meet the others.

DUNGEON

Mark, Stingas and Johnson are creeping silently along the passageway leading to the dungeon. There are two guards standing at the entrance while a third guard is pacing up and down the passageway; with the dungeon key hanging from his belt.

Stingas

I will go for the guard with the key; you and Johnson should go for the other two guards (*whispering to Mark*)

Stingas swerves his hand in the air and a sword appears in his hands. Johnson and Mark do the same.

Mark

Stingas, I think you should hide your sword and distract them first

Johnson

Brilliant idea

Stingas swerves his hand and his sword disappears. He walks toward the guards.

Stingas

Good day guards. Have you by any chance seen my brother around here? (*talking to the guards*)

Guard 1

No ….. not at all but anyway, you are not allowed to come around here

Stingas

You think so?

He swerves his hands and his sword appears in his hands again. He raises his sword to strike the guard who instantaneously strikes back. The two of them parry with their swords.

Guard 1

Are you crazy?

Mark and Johnson leap out of their hiding place; the other guards see them and attack. For a few minutes, there is a melee with sword striking sword.

SOUTHERN DOOR

Amanda arrives at the basement and sees Fergie, Joey and Kelly waiting.

Amanda

Where are the others?

Joey

They went to rescue the human captives from the dungeon

Fergie

What happened?

Kelly

Have you unlocked the basement?

Amanda

Yes, I did….. hasn't it opened yet?

Fergie

It hasn't

Amanda

Oh my God, maybe I picked the wrong bracelet!

Kelly

What are you talking about?

Amanda

The king has two bracelets. I got confused when I was about to make the swap; I couldn't remember which one had been on his left wrist

DUNGEON

Stingas strikes the patrol guard on the neck and he falls. While Mark and Johnson fight with the other two guards, Stingas quickly removes the key from the patrol guard's belt and hurries to the dungeon gate. Mark and Johnson both conquer the remaining guards, striking them down. Stingas unlocks the dungeon gate and runs inside with Mark and Johnson close behind him.

Stingas

Don't be afraid! We are also humans although disguised as Gatalinans. We have been able to open the doorway to earth. Hurry up! Go towards the backyard through the southern door (*he yells*)

The human captives start to rush out through the wide open gates.

PALACE BACKYARD

Amanda is looking distraught, thinking that the mission has failed. Kelly, Joey and Fergie are sitting forlornly on the ground. Suddenly there is a cracking sound behind them. They all turn around immediately.

Fergie

The basement is opening!

Amanda

Oooh! It worked (*she cries in relief*)

Fergie

Let's go in, right away

Joey

No way! We are not leaving without the others

Suddenly they hear a roaring noise behind them and when they turn around, they see a crowd of people running towards them with Johnson, Mark and Stingas leading.

Kelly

They have been rescued (*she claps her hands*)

As the mob runs towards the backyard, a troop of soldiers numbering about one hundred and led by Lieutenant Krols comes running to intercept them. As both groups meet, they stop running and stand glaring at each other.

Krols

Stop there! Not so fast …… I knew and I could have sworn that your people were impostors *(pointing at Mark, Johnson and Stingas who are standing abreast of the mob)*

The captives are edging back but Mark, Johnson and Stingas stand still with their swords in their hands.

Stingas

Give way (*as he takes a step forward*)

Krols smiles in amusement.

Krols

And what are you going to do? Fight a hundred soldiers? (*he laughs*)

With Krols still laughing, Stingas suddenly launches an attack on the soldiers. Mark and Johnson follow suit.

They fight the soldiers with rage and then their swords begin to glow red. The blades of their swords become red hot and they fight with confidence, knocking down several soldiers at once with just one swish of the sword.

The mob is at a distance watching the three fight. All of a sudden, a man in the mob turns to his fellow captives and shouts ……..

Man

These men are fighting for our freedom! Are we just going to stand there and watch while they fight? Come on, let's fight for liberty!

Another man from the crowd replies:

Man 2

We would love to but we have no weapons and we are still bound with chains

While he is yet speaking, there is a sound of a great wind blowing. Instantly, the chains begin to break and fall off the captives and as they become free, swords begin to appear in their hands. There are shouts of amazement.

Man 2

Yes! Now let's fight

The mob roars in anger and in one accord, they all rush into the midst of the soldiers and begin to fight. As they fight with rage, their swords begin to glow red and the blades become red-hot.

The battle rages on with many soldiers being killed and a few captives also dying. Servants and workers in the palace run around helter-skelter for safety; the entire palace is in chaos.

Amanda

Let's go assist them

Amanda and the others run towards the mob. When they get there, Fergie and Joey swerve their hands one after the other and swords appear in their hands. They join in the fight and their swords also start to glow. Amanda and Kelly stand back and shout words of encouragement. The fight continues for several more minutes.

BASEMENT

The basement door begins to close slowly, making a loud cracking sound as it moves.

Amanda

The basement! It's closing

Let's go! (*she screams*)

By this time, many of the soldiers have been killed and only a few are left.

Mark

Amanda, you and Kelly need to start leading the people to the basement (*as he strikes a soldier down*)

Amanda

We are not going without you guys

Mark

Don't worry; we will join you very soon. Just go! Go!

Kelly

Watch your back, Mark! (*screaming*)

A soldier is about to strike Mark from behind but just in time, one of the captives comes from behind the soldier and strikes the soldier on the head before he can strike Mark. Mark turns around in time to see what is happening.

Mark

Thank you (*looking at the man who saved him who nods in acknowledgement*)

Johnson

Go Amanda!

Amanda and Kelly turn round and head towards the basement.

Stingas

Follow them (*to the captives*)

The captives begin to run after Amanda and Kelly. Some of the few soldiers left try to block their way; they kill some of the captives but most of them are able to escape the soldiers. Fergie and Joey also head towards the basement.

Stingas

Go Johnson!

Johnson

Are you sure you will be alright?

Stingas

Don't worry about me, just go

Johnson also heads towards the basement, looking up at the sky as he goes. The watery clouds are getting dark like it is about to rain heavily and it has become very windy. The birds in the sky hurry back to their nests while the citizens of Gatalina race back to their respective homes; some on flying brooms, some on dragons and some on foot. The entire kingdom is in a start of chaos.

ON THE KING'S JOURNEY

The king's entourage notices the change in the clouds and the approaching storm. General Speckles who is leading the entourage stops his dragon and all the escorts also stop.

Speckles

Something has gone wrong (*he beckons at the sky*)

The king looks out through the window of the chariot to see what is going on. He looks up and sees the dark clouds which now have ripples swirling on them. He instantly bends his head to examine the bracelet on his left wrist and cries out in rage as he realizes that it is Princess Samake's.

King

I will have Amanda's head tonight. Take me back to the palace! (*he yells*)

The entourage makes a U-turn and heads back to the palace at full speed. The king's chariot swerves left and right as they dash away in the air.

SAMAKE'S BEDROOM

Princess Samake is sitting on the floor in a corner, crying and sweating profusely. There is a bang on the door; it is her friend Sonetta. The princess blocks her ears with her hands and does not respond.

SOUTHERN DOOR

Only five soldiers are left standing, including Krols. They continue to attack Mark and Stingas who both have cuts and wounds all over their bodies. Mark and Stingas fight back.

BASEMENT

The basement door is now closed quarter ways. Amanda and Kelly arrive at the edge and look into each other's eyes.

Amanda

Come on!

Kelly

What if this basement is a trap?

While they stand there hesitating, some of the captives that were behind them begin to jump into the basement without faltering. Amanda grabs Kelly's hand and jumps in, pulling Kelly along with her. More captives arrive and jump into the basement.

PALACE ENTRANCE

The king and his entourage arrive at the palace; and he jumps off the carriage even before it stops. He lands on the ground on his two feet and draws his sword as he runs into the palace. Speckles and the other soldiers (hundreds of them) also barge into the palace, following the king who is roaring in anger and fuming with rage.

SOUTHERN DOOR

Mark strikes down the last soldier (except Krols) and hurries towards the basement.

Mark

Let's go Stingas! More soldiers are coming

Stingas is in a tough sword fight with Krols who is a very strong fighter. Mark looks back and upon seeing Krols almost killing Stingas, he turns back to help.

Stingas

No, go! Don't worry

Mark hesitates.

Stingas contd

Gooooo! (*he grunts as he swings his sword at Krols*)

The king and the soldiers are running towards the southern door. Mark starts running to the basement and Stingas is the only human left.

Stingas sees the king and his entourage coming and with all his strength, he swings his sword to parry Krols's sword which falls off Krols's hand. Stingas then plunges his sword into Krols's chest.

Krols groans in pain as he falls slowly to his knees and then to the ground.

Stingas runs towards the basement with King Mapheononicus, General Speckles and scores of soldiers running after him.

Mark gets to the basement. Few captives are still diving into the basement. He gets to the edge, pauses and looks back. He smiles as he sights Stingas emerging from the southern door, approaching the basement. Mark suddenly stops smiling as he sees the king and his men running behind Stingas.

Mark

Hurry! They are coming behind you!

The last two captives (a mother and son) jump into the basement.

Stingas

Go! Mark, just go!

Mark takes a dive into the basement. The basement door is almost completely closed; the span of the opening is about two feet and it is closing gradually.

Stingas finally gets to the edge and he turns around to face the king and his men.

Stingas

Goodbye forever!

He waves and smiles as he takes a dive into the almost closed basement. Furious, the king swings his sword at Stingas with a shout but it misses him by inches as he disappears through the opening.

The basement door closes shut.

King

NOOOOOOOOOOOOOOOO!!!!!!!!!!!!
(*he screams*)

BLACK OUT!

AUTHOR'S BIO

AUTHOR'S BIO

FEMI ONI is the last born child of a family of three. He was born on the 24th of June 1988 in Oyo State, Nigeria but he hails from Abeokuta, Ogun State. He studied Industrial Chemistry at the Federal University of Technology Akure.

Femi's interest in fantasy and adventure stories started right from his childhood when he started reading fairytales. He later decided to start writing his own books; greatly inspired by books such as The Lord of the Rings and the Harry Potter series.

Femi has always loved and has been a fan of fantasy adventure stories and 'Bermuda Triangle' is his first completed work even though he has written many unfinished stories.

Contact Information

Korloki Publishing Company

1320 Coney Island Avenue Suite B3

Brooklyn, NY 11230

Email: authors@kpcbooks.com

Website:

www.kpcbooks.com

www.ingramcontent.com/pod-product-compliance
Lightning Source LLC
Chambersburg PA
CBHW071652160426
43195CB00012B/1436